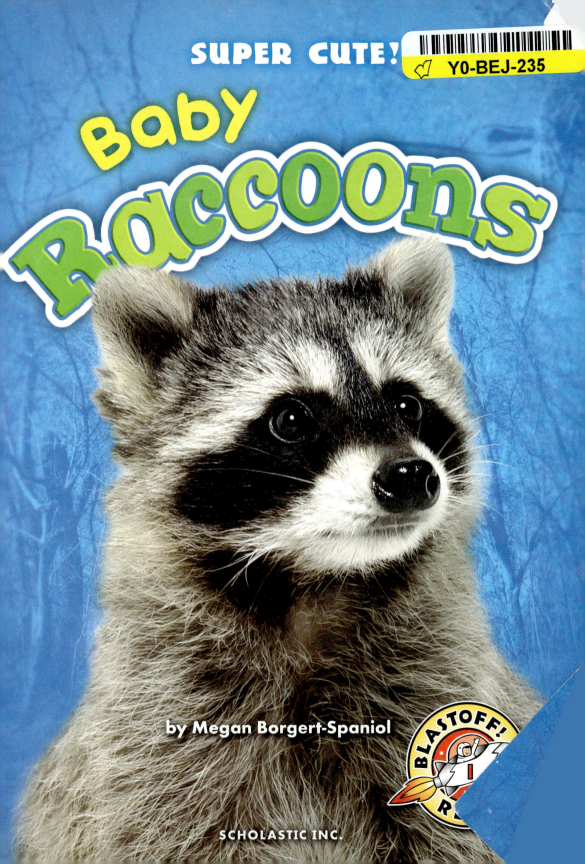

SUPER CUTE!

YO-BEJ-235

Baby
Raccoons

by Megan Borgert-Spaniol

SCHOLASTIC INC.

Note to Librarians, Teachers, and Parents:

Blastoff! Readers are carefully developed by literacy experts and combine standards-based content with developmentally appropriate text.

Level 1 provides the most support through repetition of high-frequency words, light text, predictable sentence patterns, and strong visual support.

Level 2 offers early readers a bit more challenge through varied simple sentences, increased text load, and less repetition of high-frequency words.

Level 3 advances early-fluent readers toward fluency through increased text and concept load, less reliance on visuals, longer sentences, and more literary language.

Level 4 builds reading stamina by providing more text per page, increased use of punctuation, greater variation in sentence patterns, and increasingly challenging vocabulary.

Level 5 encourages children to move from "learning to read" to "reading to learn" by providing even more text, varied writing styles, and less familiar topics.

Whichever book is right for your reader, Blastoff! Readers are the perfect books to build confidence and encourage a love of reading that will last a lifetime!

ISBN 978-1-338-22331-6

Text copyright © 2017 by Bellwether Media, Inc. All rights reserved. Published by Scholastic Inc., 557 Broadway, New York, NY 10012, by arrangement with Bellwether Media, Inc. BLASTOFF! READERS and associated logos are trademarks and/or registered trademarks of Bellwether Media, Inc. SCHOLASTIC and associated logos are trademarks and/or registered trademarks of Scholastic Inc.

12 11 10 9 8 7 6 5 4 3 2 1   17 18 19 20 21 22

Printed in the U.S.A.   40

First Scholastic printing, September 2017

Editor: Betsy Rathburn
Designer: Brittany McIntosh

Table of Contents

Raccoon Cubs!

Baby raccoons are called cubs. There are up to seven cubs in a **litter**.

Newborn cubs cannot see or hear for three weeks. They **nurse** inside their **den**.

Outside the Den

In two months, the cubs are ready to explore. They peek outside their den.

The cubs stay close together. They like to **wrestle** and play.

Their mom protects them from danger. She watches for **predators**.

Sometimes mom carries the cubs in her mouth.

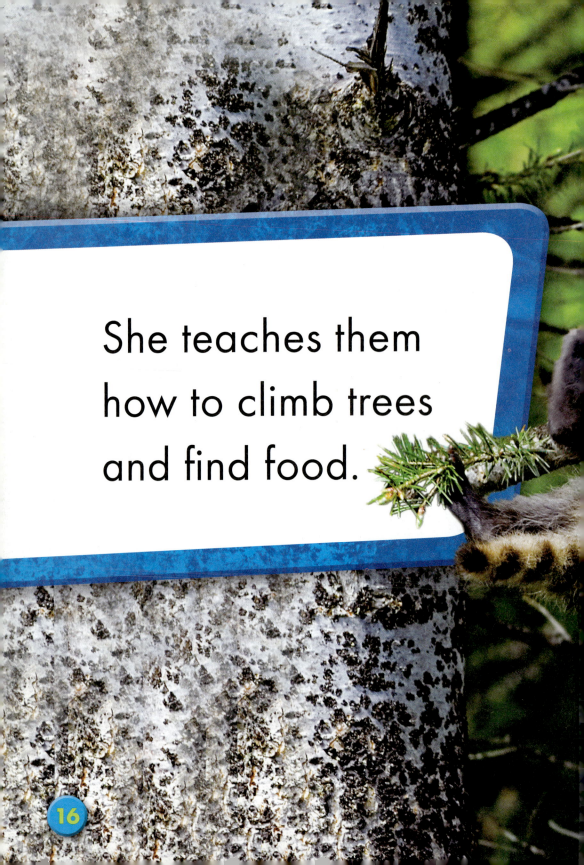

She teaches them how to climb trees and find food.

Finding Food

Now the cubs can **forage** with mom. They eat plants, nuts, and small animals.

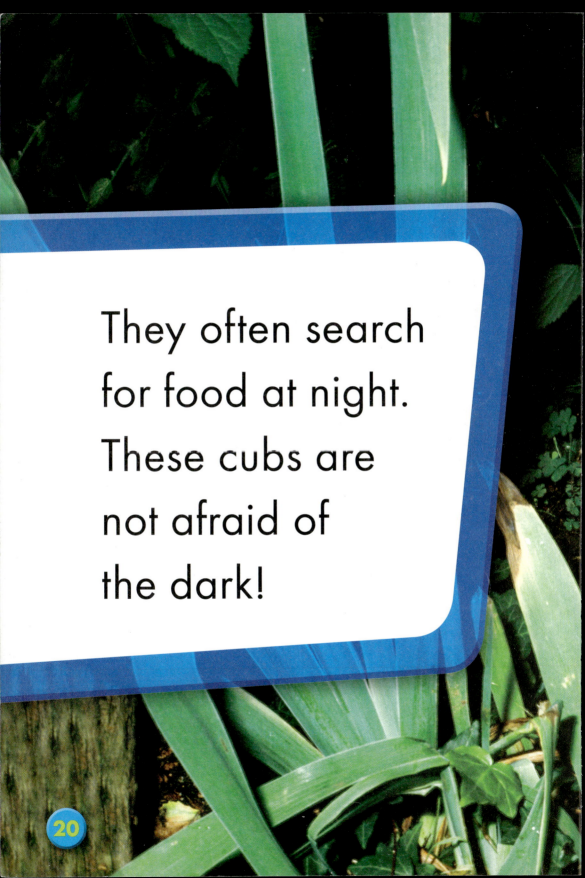

They often search for food at night. These cubs are not afraid of the dark!

Glossary

den—the place where raccoon cubs are born and raised

forage—to go out in search of food

litter—a group of babies that are born together

newborn—just recently born

nurse—to drink mom's milk

predators—animals that hunt other animals for food

wrestle—to fight in a playful way

To Learn More

AT THE LIBRARY

Green, Emily K. *Raccoons.* Minneapolis, Minn.: Bellwether Media, 2011.

Johnson, J. Angelique. *Raccoons.* Mankato, Minn.: Capstone Press, 2011.

Penn, Audrey. *A Bedtime Kiss for Chester Raccoon.* Terre Haute, Ind.: Tanglewood, 2010.

Index